SPELLING FOR MINECRAFTERS

Grade 2

Illustrated by Amanda Brack

Sky Pony Press
New York

Sky Pony Press books may be purchased in bulk at special discounts for sales promotion, corporate gifts, fund-raising, or educational purposes. Special editions can also be created to specifications. For details, contact the Special Sales Department, Sky Pony Press, 307 West 36th Street, 11th Floor, New York, NY 10018 or info@skyhorsepublishing.com.

Sky Pony® is a registered trademark of Skyhorse Publishing, Inc.®, a Delaware corporation.

Visit our website at www.skyponypress.com.

10 9 8 7 6 5 4 3 2

Library of Congress Cataloging-in-Publication Data is available on file.

Cover design by Bill Greenhead

Cover illustration by Bill Greenhead

Interior illustrations by Amanda Brack and Bill Greenhead

Book design by Kevin Baier

Print ISBN: 978-1-5107-3766-2

Printed in the United States of America

A NOTE TO PARENTS

When you want to reinforce classroom skills at home, it's crucial to have kid-friendly learning materials. This *Spelling for Minecrafters* workbook transforms spelling practice into an irresistible adventure, complete with diamond swords, zombies, skeletons, and creepers. That means less arguing over homework and more fun overall.

Spelling for Minecrafters is also fully aligned with National Common Core Standards for 2nd-grade spelling. What does that mean, exactly? All of the spelling skills taught in this book correspond to what your child is expected to learn in school. This eliminates confusion and builds confidence for greater homework-time success!

Whether it's the joy of seeing their favorite game characters on every page or the thrill of spelling with Steve and Alex, there is something in this workbook to entice even the most reluctant speller.

Happy adventuring!

MISSING LETTERS

*What letters are missing from the **bossy r (r-controlled)** words below? Choose **ar, er, ir, or,** or **ur**. Write the full word on the line with the added letters underlined.*

1. f _ _ m

2. f _ _ ry

3. d _ _ t

4. h _ _ se

5. b _ _ k

6. flow _ _

WORD FILL-IN

*Use the box of **bossy r (r-controlled)** words to finish the sentences below.*

art	cart	dark	hard	park

1. Steve goes for at ride in the _____.

2. He stops for a picnic lunch at the _____.

3. Then Steve goes to a museum to check out some _____.

4. On the way home the cart hits something _____.

5. Hurry home, Steve, before it gets _____!

SIGHT WORD WRITING CHALLENGE

Practice spelling the sight words below. As you write the letters, say them out loud.

1. only

2. new

3. take

4. little

5. know

6. place

STORY MAKER

Write a few sentences about Minecraft using as many of the sight words below as you can.

know	new	little	only	place	take

FIND AND FIX

Look for one spelling mistake in each sentence below. Cross out the mistake and write the word correctly on the line.

1. Do you knaw how to get to the End?

_____

_____

2. Look out for zombies when it's durk.

_____

_____

3. Although baby zombies are littel,

they can still do a lot of damage.

_____

_____

4. Tak a boat to travel by sea quickly.

_____

_____

5. Riding a hores may be the fastest way

to travel in Survival mode.

_____

 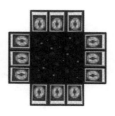 

WITHER'S WORD SEARCH

Can you find and circle all the words from the list?

art	bark	cart	dark
farm	flower	furry	hard
horse	know	little	new
only	park	place	take
			dirt

```
T R I D E R K E B W
R E Y H E L C R N X
A Y K W O A T D A N
C D O A L R K T D B
B L M P T R S R I X
F U R R Y D O E A L
K D R A H A M N N P
N T M Y N R B E L X
O R R W A K W M T Y
W A J F N X N B T K
```

WORD FILL-IN

*Use the box of **-ight** words to finish the sentences below.*

right	might	sight	flight	bright

1. The bat took _____ .

2. It flew _____ into lava.

3. It was quite a _____ to see!

4. You never know what you _____ discover

in Minecraft.

5. Keep your _____ eyes open.

STEVE'S WORD SCRAMBLE

*Unscramble the **-ight** words below. Write them correctly on the line.*

1. ghnit

2. tshig

3. irgbht

4. hftgi

5. lhigtf

SIGHT WORD WRITING CHALLENGE

Practice spelling the sight words below. As you write the letters, say them out loud.

1. very

2. after

3. things

4. life

5. great

6. help

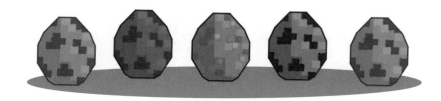

STORY MAKER

Write a few sentences about Minecraft using as many of the sight words below as you can.

very	after	things	life	great	help

FIND AND FIX

Look for one spelling mistake in each sentence below. Cross out the mistake and write the word correctly on the line.

1. My friend is veery skilled at Minecraft.

2. It's fun to watch him figt a mob.

3. Affter we play Minecraft, we like to pretend we have entered the game.

4. Imagine Minecraft really came to lief.

5. Would you be afraid to go out at nite?

WORD CRAFTING

*Alex opened an enchanted chest and found these letters. Help her craft as many **-ight** words as you can. Write them below.*

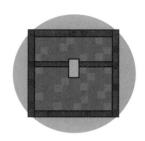

s   t   f

b   h

m   n

l   r

g   i

1. _____

2. _____

3. _____

4. _____

5. _____

6. _____

7. _____

8. _____

9. _____

10. _____

11. _____

12. _____

MISSING LETTERS

*What vowel teams are missing from the words below? Choose **ou** or **ue**. Write the full word on the line with the added letters underlined.*

1. Alex f ___ ___ nd a cocoa plant.

2. The potion is bl ___ ___ .

3. The music is l ___ ___ d.

4. C ___ ___ nt the blocks.

5. Here is a cl ___ ___ to defeat guardians.

SIGHT WORD WRITING CHALLENGE

Practice spelling the sight words below. As you write the letters, say them out loud.

1. before

2. soon

3. want

4. any

5. large

6. does

WITHER'S WORD SEARCH

Can you find and circle all the words from the list?

argue	any	before	blue
count	does	due	found
glue	large	loud	round
shout	soon	true	want
			clue

B C D A S D N J W A N T
E A O O N O B L U E K N
F X R U E Y O L R R K X
O M O G N S W N E N G T
R F N G U T M G D T R L
E P L L L E R N E J M N
S H O U T A U U C L U E
M L U E L O R D U E B V
R R D Z R T Z L R Q Y T

STORY MAKER

Write a few sentences about Minecraft using as many of the words from the search's word bank (**page 16**) as you can.

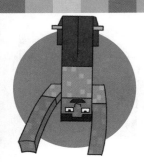

STEVE'S WORD SCRAMBLE

*Unscramble the sight words below. Write them correctly on the line. Use **page 15** for help if you need it.*

1. nawt

2. noos

3. orbfee

4. esdo

5. yan

6. greal

WORD FILL-IN

*Use the box of **ou** and **ue** words to finish the sentences below.*

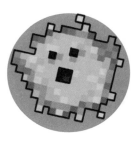

round	due	true	glue	argue

1. Do you think the legend of Herobrine is _____?

2. Building something _____ in Minecraft is challenging.

3. My friends _____ about which video game is the best.

4. The Minecraft book I borrowed from the library is _____ to be returned.

5. You can make _____ in mods to stick slabs together.

LONG AND SHORT VOWELS

Fill in the missing vowel team to complete the word. Circle **long** *or* **short** *to describe the sound the vowel makes.*

1. br___ ___d   **LONG**   **SHORT**

2. dr___ ___m   **LONG**   **SHORT**

3.  p___ ___k   **LONG**   **SHORT**

4. h___ ___d   **LONG**   **SHORT**

5. m___ ___t   **LONG**   **SHORT**

WORD FILL-IN

*Use the box of **ea** words to finish the sentences below. Circle long or short to describe the sound the vowel makes.*

beat	Beach	team	dead	seat

1. You will find sand in a _____ Biome.

LONG
SHORT

2. If you get tired of walking, you can make a _____.

LONG
SHORT

3. Join with other players as a _____.

LONG
SHORT

4. Zombies are easy to _____ with sunlight.

LONG
SHORT

5. When you have no health points left, you are _____.

LONG
SHORT

SIGHT WORD WRITING CHALLENGE

Practice spelling the sight words below. As you write the letters, say them out loud.

1. another

2. even

3. color

4. shape

5. because

6. here

FIND AND FIX

Look for one spelling mistake in each sentence below. Cross out the mistake and write the word correctly on the line.

1. Imagine if Steve and Alex could live hear.

   _____

2. I found anouther diamond.

   _____

3. Check to make sure your walls are evan.

   _____

4. I'm using a torch, becus I need more light.

   _____

5. How many coler codes do you know?

   _____

WITHER'S WORD SEARCH

Can you find and circle all the words from the list?

another	beach	beat	because
bread	color	dead	dream
even	head	here	meat
peak	seat	shape	team

```
M R C S E A T D N M Q P R
E Y J O B T M T B D T Y L
A P Y V L T Y T M J M Y Y
T P E P X O T E V E N Z D
P R B A B V R E S J L J R
M J B E K E W U A W J E Y
W W Q R A R A P K M H M D
S T D Y E C B T N T Q Y L
H H R R E A H D O X E T K
A E M B E N D N E R L G T
P A D P Z A A D E A R N X
E D K L P B M H Z R D Y V
```

STORY MAKER

*Write a few sentences about Minecraft using as many of the words from the search's word bank (**page 24**) as you can.*

ENDING BLENDS

What letters are missing from the words below? Write the full word on the line with the added letters underlined. Use the word bank below to help.

chest	blast	sand	craft	fast

1. bla _ _ _____

2. sa _ _ _____

3. fa _ _ _____

4. che _ _ _____

5. cra _ _ _____

WORD FILL-IN

Use the box of words with **ending blends** to finish the sentences below.

camp	test	jump	mind	wind

1. Donkeys can't _____ as high as horses.

2. Survival maps _____ your fighting and survival skills.

3. We built a great _____ site with a fire pit.

4. If a villager stops accepting a trade, trade other items until he changes his _____ .

5. You can make waves and _____ with mods.

SIGHT WORD WRITING CHALLENGE

Practice spelling the sight words below. As you write the letters, say them out loud.

1. food

2. body

3. build

4. went

5. read

6. size

STEVE'S WORD SCRAMBLE

*Unscramble the sight words below. Write them correctly on the line. Use **page 28** for help if you need it.*

1. netw _____

2. ubldi _____

3. dofo _____

4. yodb _____

5. zies _____

6. drea _____

WITHER'S WORD SEARCH

Can you find and circle all the words from the list?

blast	body	build	camp
chest	craft	fast	food
jump	mind	read	sand
size	test	went	wind

P Y D O B T S A F J
M L T T P D S O T T
U D F B A M O A N D
J D A E T D A E L Z
R M R M T S W C M B
T L C E T B I I J T
L P S M S M U Z N L
B T I L E A D I E D
D N D L H T N R L N
D P W Q C V L D V D

STORY MAKER

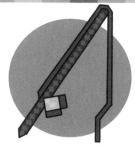

*Write a few sentences about Minecraft using as many of the words from the search's word bank (**page 30**) as you can.*

ENDING BLENDS

What letters are missing from the words below? Write the full word on the line with the added letters underlined. Use the word bank below to help.

clock	church	block	torch	bush

1. blo _ _

2. clo _ _

3. tor _ _

4. bu _ _

5. chur _ _

WORD FILL-IN

*Use the box of words with **ending blends** to finish the sentences below.*

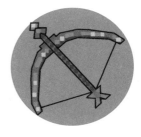

much	wish	search	rich	rush

1. It is _____ easier to beat the Wither with

the help of friends.

2. He is _____ in iron, gold, and diamonds.

3. What do you _____ for in new Minecraft

releases?

4. It is fun to explore and _____ for new

biomes.

5. To fight blazes, use Fire Resistance potions and

_____ them as they start to rise in the air.

SIGHT WORD WRITING CHALLENGE

Practice spelling the sight words below. As you write the letters, say them out loud.

1. animal

2. fire

3. home

4. move

5. love

6. try

STEVE'S WORD SCRAMBLE

*Unscramble the sight words below. Write them correctly on the line. Use **page 34** for help if you need it.*

1. omhe

2. veom

3. voel

4. mlania

5. ifre

6. ytr

WITHER'S WORD SEARCH

Can you find and circle all the words from the list?

again	animal	block	bush
church	clock	fire	home
love	move	much	rich
rush	search	torch	try
			wish

```
A R U S H H D D D H
S N J N C W G X C D
E T I R M K I R Q Y
A D U M C O O S R T
R H C O A T V T H E
C R L J G L E E V D
H B O H A R H O P H
L N C R I I L O S T
M U K F N C D U M Y
M R L R Z H B L Z E
```

WORD CRAFTING

Alex opened an enchanted chest and found these letters.
Help her craft as many words with **ending blends** as you can.
Write them below.

b   h   t

w   c

m   o

i

r   s   u

1. _____

2. _____

3. _____

4. _____

5. _____

6. _____

7. _____

8. _____

9. _____

10. _____

11. _____

12. _____

WORD FILL-IN

*Use the box of **wh-** words to finish the sentences below. Be sure to include capital letters at the start of sentences.*

white	While	whirl	Whale	whip

1. _____s are passive mobs that can only be obtained through mods.

2. _____ the Nether can seem scary, you can stay safe with armor and weapons.

3. Silverfish can swarm and _____ around you to do a lot of damage quickly.

4. Horses can be one of seven colors: _____, buckskin, bay, dark bay, black, chestnut, and gray.

5. The _____ is a tool in some mods that can be used to stop mobs from moving.

STEVE'S WORD SCRAMBLE

*Unscramble the **wh-** words below. Write them correctly on the line.*

1. nehw

2. ewerh

3. awht

4. yhw

5. hcwih

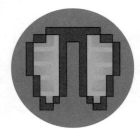

SIGHT WORD WRITING CHALLENGE

Practice spelling the sight words below. As you write the letters, say them out loud.

1. should

2. learn

3. find

4. write

5. problem

6. select

STORY MAKER

Write a few sentences about Minecraft using as many of the sight words below as you can

should	learn	find	write	problem	select

FIND AND FIX

Look for one spelling mistake in each sentence below. Cross out the mistake and write the word correctly on the line. Don't forget to capitalize at the beginning of sentences.

1. You can tell wen a spider is nearby because of its hiss.

2. Whare are you building your farm?

3. Wat is your favorite biome?

4. I often think about what additions Minecraft shud make.

5. An iron axe has a durability of 251, wich means you can use it 251 times.

WORD CRAFTING

Alex opened an enchanted chest and found these letters. Help her craft as many **wh-** words as you can. Write them below.

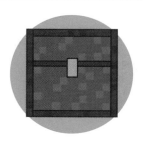

n
c   e   r
h   l
                            e
w   r

i   e
y   t   a   h

1. _____

2. _____

3. _____

4. _____

5. _____

6. _____

7. _____

8. _____

9. _____

10. _____

11. _____

12. _____

MISSING LETTERS

*What **letter team** is missing from all of the words below? Write the full word on the line with the added letters underlined.*

1. Br__ __ __ along blocks to bridge to the End.

2. Place a r__ __ __ of glass blocks around the sapling.

3. Look at the bat's w__ __ __ .

4. Fletchers buy str__ __ __ and sell bows.

5. Use a special suit to protect yourself from a bee st__ __ __.

STEVE'S WORD SCRAMBLE

*Unscramble the **-ing** words below. Write them correctly on the line.*

1. gisn

2. gnki

3. lsgin

4. gicln

5. prgsni

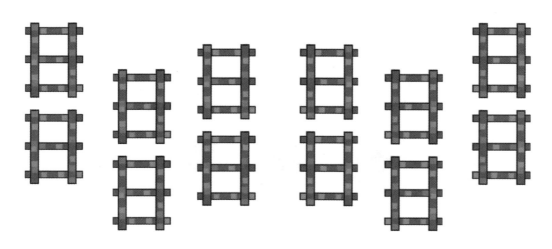

SIGHT WORD WRITING CHALLENGE

Practice spelling the sight words below. As you write the letters, say them out loud.

1. age

2. minute

3. hour

4. greater

5. equal

6. question

STORY MAKER

Write a few sentences about Minecraft using as many of the sight words below as you can.

age	minute	hour	greater	equal	question

WITHER'S WORD SEARCH

Can you find and circle all the words from the list?

age	bring	cling	equal
greater	hour	king	minute
question	ring	sing	sling
spring	sting	string	wing

```
B S L Q X T R N G T P J
R L R X M E O N J N L D
I I A N T I I C L I N G
N N G A T T N Q G L X T
G G E S S Y G U A Q R B
Q R E G T N Q U T G J N
G U N R I R Q M N E B T
Q I U R J E I I K I N G
S O P W B D R N W I N G
H S Y Y L B R P G N V B
```

48

WORD CRAFTING

*Alex opened an enchanted chest and found these letters. Help her craft as many **-ing** words as you can. Write them below.*

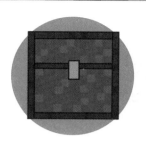

k   s   r

g

b

n

w

i

l

p   c   t

1. _____

2. _____

3. _____

4. _____

5. _____

6. _____

7. _____

8. _____

9. _____

10. _____

11. _____

12. _____

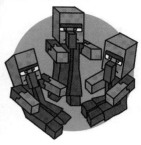

SIGHT WORD REVIEW: COPY AND LEARN

Copy the words on the lines provided.

1. only

2. new

3. take

4. little

5. know

6. place

7. very

8. after

9. things

10. life

11. great

12. help

SPELLING TEST 1: SIGHT WORDS

*Time to do some wordcrafting! Have a parent or friend read the words from **page 50** to you and see how many you can spell correctly.*

Date: _____

Number correct: _____

1. _____

2. _____

3. _____

4. _____

5. _____

6. _____

7. _____

8. _____

9. _____

10. _____

11. _____

12. _____

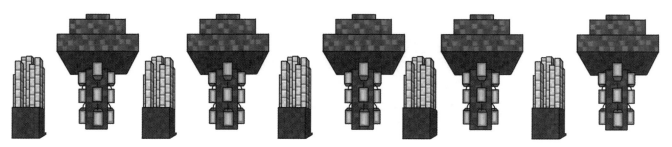

SIGHT WORD REVIEW: COPY AND LEARN

Copy the words on the lines provided.

1. before

2. soon

3. want

4. any

5. large

6. does

7. another

8. even

9. color

10. shape

11. because

12. here

SPELLING TEST 2: SIGHT WORDS

*Time to do some wordcrafting! Have a parent or friend read the words from **page 52** to you and see how many you can spell correctly.*

Date: _____

Number correct: _____

1. _____

2. _____

3. _____

4. _____

5. _____

6. _____

7. _____

8. _____

9. _____

10. _____

11. _____

12. _____

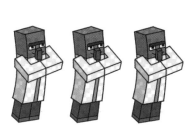

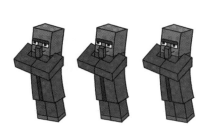

SIGHT WORD REVIEW: COPY AND LEARN

Copy the words on the lines provided.

1. food

2. body

3. build

4. went

5. read

6. size

7. animal

8. fire

9. home

10. move

11. love

12. try

SPELLING TEST 3: SIGHT WORDS

*Time to do some wordcrafting! Have a parent or friend read the words from **page 54** to you and see how many you can spell correctly.*

Date: _____

Number correct: _____

1. _____

2. _____

3. _____

4. _____

5. _____

6. _____

7. _____

8. _____

9. _____

10. _____

11. _____

12. _____

SIGHT WORD REVIEW: COPY AND LEARN

Copy the words on the lines provided.

1. should

2. learn

3. find

4. write

5. problem

6. select

7. greater

8. equal

9. hour

10. minute

11. age

12. question

SPELLING TEST 4: SIGHT WORDS

*Time to do some wordcrafting! Have a parent or friend read the words from **page 56** to you and see how many you can spell correctly.*

Date: ....

Number correct: ....

1. ....

2. ....

3. ....

4. ....

5. ....

6. ....

7. ....

8. ....

9. ....

10. ....

11. ....

12. ....

ANSWERS

PAGE 2, MISSING LETTERS

1) f**a**rm
2) f**u**ry
3) d**ir**t
4) h**or**se
5) b**ar**k
6) flow**er**

PAGE 3, WORD FILL-IN

1) cart
2) park
3) art
4) hard
5) dark

PAGE 6, FIND AND FIX

1) know
2) dark
3) little
4) Take
5) horse

PAGE 7, WITHER'S WORD SEARCH

```
T R I D E R K E B W
R E Y H E L C R N X
A Y K W O A T D A N
C D O A L R K T D B
B L M P T R S R I X
F U R R Y D O E A L
K D R A H A M N N P
N T M Y N R B E L X
O R R W A K W M T Y
W A J F N X N B T K
```

PAGE 8, WORD FILL-IN

1) flight
2) right
3) sight
4) might
5) bright

PAGE 9, STEVE'S WORD SCRAMBLE

1) night
2) sight
3) bright
4) fight
5) flight

PAGE 12, FIND AND FIX

1) very
2) fight
3) After
4) life
5) night

PAGE 13, WORD CRAFTING

Answers may vary. Some answers include: bright, fight, flight, light, might, night, right, sight

PAGE 14, MISSING LETTERS

1) f**ou**nd
2) bl**ue**
3) l**ou**d
4) C**ou**nt
5) cl**ue**

PAGE 16, WITHER'S WORD SEARCH

```
B C D A S D N J W A N T
E A O O N O B L U E K N
F X R U E Y O L R R K X
O M O G N S W N E N G T
R F N G U T M G D T R L
E P L L E R N E J M N
S H O U T A U U C L U E
M L U E L O R D U E B V
R R D Z R T Z L R Q Y T
```

PAGE 18, STEVE'S WORD SCRAMBLE

1) want
2) soon
3) before
4) does
5) any
6) large

PAGE 19, WORD FILL-IN

1) true
2) round
3) argue
4) due
5) glue

PAGE 20, LONG AND SHORT VOWELS

1) br**ea**d (short)
2) dr**ea**m (long)
3) p**ea**k (long)
4) h**ea**d (short)
5) m**ea**t (long)

PAGE 21, WORD FILL-IN

1) B**ea**ch (long)
2) s**ea**t (long)
3) t**ea**m (long)
4) b**ea**t (long)
5) d**ea**d (short)

PAGE 23, FIND AND FIX

1) here
2) another
3) even
4) because
5) color

PAGE 24, WITHER'S WORD SEARCH

```
M R C S E A T D N M Q P R
E Y J O B T M T B D T Y L
A P Y V L T Y T M J M Y Y
T P E P X O T E V E N Z D
P R B A B V R E S J L J R
M J B E K E W U A W J E Y
W W Q R A R A P K M H M D
S T D Y E C B T N T Q Y L
H R R R E A H D O X E T K
A E M B E N D N E R L G T
P A D P Z A A D E A R N X
E D K L P B M H Z R D Y V
```

PAGE 26, ENDING BLENDS

1) bla**st**
2) sa**nd**
3) fa**st**
4) che**st**
5) cra**ft**

PAGE 27, WORD FILL-IN

1) jump
2) test
3) camp
4) mind
5) wind

PAGE 29, STEVE'S WORD SCRAMBLE

1) went
2) build
3) food
4) body
5) size
6) read

PAGE 30, WITHER'S WORD SEARCH

```
P Y D O B T S A F J
M L T T P D S O T T
U D F B A M O A N D
J D A E T D A E L Z
R M R M T S W C M B
T L C E T B I I J T
L P S M S M U Z N L
B T I L E A D I E D
D N D L H T N R L N
D P W Q C V L D V D
```

PAGE 32, ENDING BLENDS

1) blo<u>ck</u>
2) clo<u>ck</u>
3) tor<u>ch</u>
4) bu<u>sh</u>
5) chur<u>ch</u>

PAGE 33, WORD FILL-IN

1) much
2) rich
3) wish
4) search
5) rush

PAGE 35, STEVE'S WORD SCRAMBLE

1) home
2) move
3) love
4) animal
5) fire
6) try

PAGE 36, WITHER'S WORD SEARCH

```
A R U S H H D D D H
S N J N C W G X C D
E T I R M K I R Q Y
A D U M C O O S R T
R H C O A T V T H E
C R L J G L E E V D
H B O H A R H O P H
L N C R I I L O S T
M U K F N C D U M Y
M R L R Z H B L Z E
```

PAGE 37, WORD CRAFTING

Answers may vary. Some answers include: bush, much, rich, rush, such, torch, touch, wish

PAGE 38, WORD FILL-IN

1) Whale
2) While
3) whirl
4) white
5) whip

PAGE 39, STEVE'S WORD SCRAMBLE

1) when
2) where
3) what
4) why
5) which

PAGE 42, FIND AND FIX

1) when
2) Where
3) What
4) should
5) which

PAGE 43, WORD CRAFTING

Answers may vary. Some answers include: whale, what, which, while, whirl, white, when, where, why

PAGE 44, MISSING LETTERS

1) Br<u>ing</u>
2) r<u>ing</u>
3) w<u>ing</u>
4) str<u>ing</u>
5) st<u>ing</u>

PAGE 45, STEVE'S WORD SCRAMBLE

1) sing
2) king
3) sling
4) cling
5) spring

PAGE 48, WITHER'S WORD SEARCH

```
B S L Q X T R N G T P J
R L R X M E O N J N L D
I I A N T I I C L I N G
N N G A T T N Q G L X T
G G E S S Y G U A Q R B
Q R E G T N Q U T G J N
G U N R I R Q M N E B T
Q I U R J E I I K I N G
S O P W B D R N W I N G
H S Y Y L B R P G N V B
```

PAGE 49, WORD CRAFTING

Answers may vary. Some answers include: bring, cling, king, ring, sing, sling, spring, sting, string, wing